Handyman Marketing Handbook

Your Marketing Strategy From $0 - $200K

Allen Lee

I dedicate this book to my lovely wife, Laura, and tenacious daughter, Harper! Laura, you have contantly shown me what true devotion and integrity looks like and you inspire me every day. You are one of the main reasons I do what I do! Harper, You simply never give up! You keep pressing forward and that calls me to be a better, stronger person everyday! Thank you for the incredible support in all that I do!

Table Of Contents

Foreword

In my thousands of conversations with owners of handyman and contractor businesses, I can tell you that how to successfully market is the #1 question these businesses are trying to answer - and rightly so! There are countless different opinions on "the best marketing strategies" for home service businesses. The sheer amount of information is overwhelming, and that can leave business owners feeling lost, or that they're not doing enough.

Allen Lee's Handyman Marketing Handbook cuts through the endless information and paid courses from "marketing experts" and "millionaire marketers". This practical, easy-to-understand guide will enable the reader to: understand essential marketing principles, create a foundational (and sustainable) marketing strategy, and plan for future growth.

Here are my personal favorite features of this essential handbook for any handyman or contractor business owner:

- It is written BY a handyman, FOR other handymen. Allen is not just another "marketer" trying to sell a course - he is the owner of a successful handyman business that is passing along his resources; resources that he's gathered through both his successes and failures.
- While there are recommendations for specific strategies, there is plenty of room for the reader to apply their own unique strategy (that works for them) within the framework that Allen lays out.
- This book is inspiring! Any reader that is passionate to run a successful business and learn along the way will finish this book feeling inspired, and ready to start applying what they've learned.

At the end of the day, business owners need to adapt and apply what they learn - whether through experience or education. Allen Lee's Handyman Marketing Handbook is a pivotal resource that gives actionable advice, while also leaving plenty of room for adaptation. After all, every business (and business owner) is unique.

Jason Call

Expert marketer, and Founder of

www.HandymanWebDesign.com

Introduction

When it comes to running a successful handyman business, marketing is one thing that separates the successful from the unsuccessful. Marketing is a very mysterious skill because it is all about capturing and molding the prospect's mind. In this book, you will learn how to take your handyman business from $0 to $200K if, like always, you can follow directions. This book is not one of those "ins and outs of the psychology of marketing" but rather it is the down and dirty, practical, everyday methods that I have learned through running my own successful handyman business. One major concept I will highlight in this book is how you can create, what I like to call, a Marketing Funnel to target the clients you want, have them find you, and contact YOU day and night without you pulling your hair out.

The number one thing to understand about marketing is that if you don't know what you are doing, the best thing to do is to seek out a professional in that field, do what they do, or simply let them do it for you. When you are trying to figure out whether you should let them do your marketing for you, or if you should learn from them and do it yourself, the decision really comes down to the balance between time and budget. Some people have a huge budget and not a lot of time, and if that's the case, you will be looking to hand off certain aspects of business to others. Some handymen have a whole lot of time and a small budget; these are the people who will opt to learn from the pros and do what they do.

When I first started my handyman business, I had no clue how to get my name out there, but I knew I needed to. I had no clue even where to start to find a professional to help me, so I started asking some of my friends. I found out one of my great friends actually went to school for marketing and was very gifted in that field. I then asked for some major help and learned a ton in the process. My good friend, Jason Call, has since gone on to create www.handymanwebdesign.com with the mission of helping handymen just like me reach their full potential through marketing. If you have never heard of HWD, I would highly recommend you look into it. Jason just might be the professional in the marketing field that you need to partner with.

One very important thing you need to know about marketing is that it is an investment into your business. An investment is a sacrifice now for potential success down the road, but I want you to understand that success is not guaranteed. You need to look at the money that you are about to invest as something that you are prepared to lose if that investment goes sour. Sometimes that is how investments go.

Another important matter is realizing that the marketing that you are doing now will not show full results for another 90 days - So the rule of marketing is to be patient and to start marketing now to get to where you want to be in 90 days.

Marketing Funnel - The Basics

A Marketing Funnel is a strategy that allows you to get your business in front of Ideal Clients often and directs them to reach out to you through platforms that do not require your attention 24/7. This way clients can reach you at their convenience and you can get back to them at your convenience, it's a win / win!

The Marketing Funnel can change as your business changes. My current version of the Marketing Funnel has transformed quite a bit from the one I started with. Let's start talking about the simple "starter" version and then later we will discuss the version I now use and why. When your business continues to grow, it is important for the Marketing Funnel to grow as well.

Marketing Filter

At the very top of your marketing funnel is your marketing filter. Your marketing filter is the top 5 - 10 values or core beliefs that represent your business. If presented correctly your marketing filter will allow your customers to know who your business is and what you stand for before even meeting you. The marketing filter is what all of your marketing messaging gets filtered through. So in essence, everything you say and do in marketing is filtered through to represent and show your business ideals.

Some great top core values for a business might be:
- Honor
- Integrity
- Timeliness
- Cleanliness
- Professionalism

- High quality
- Reasonably priced (Under promise and over deliver)
- Gets it done no matter what
- Admits when he doesn't know something
- Compassionate
- Has a bigger picture than just being a handyman

For our business personally, we feel called to not only be handymen and perform home repairs, but we are to be life changers and community developers.This means for our marketing filter that it has to be things like fun, caring, compassionate, professional, inspirational, life giving, willing to help even if it's something we don't do.

When you filter all of your marketing messaging through your businesses core values you do 2 things, you market to the types of clients you want and you help the clients you don't want to prescreen themselves. When one of your core values is that you do quality work and are not the cheapest in town, the people who see that advertising will understand that and qualify or disqualify themselves, thus saving you time from having to qualify them yourselves.

Your filter is portrayed through the advertisements you run, whether that is a Yelp ad or a simple Facebook post. Everything needs to portray your core values. Even the pictures you post and the wording you use, and yes even your grammar! For example, if one of your core values is professionalism then you would not want to post a picture of you working with holes in your shirt, or your pants ripped to shreds. Portraying your core values may cost you more money but believe me, it will make you far more money than it costs you! (See Marketing Filter Diagram Fig. 1 on Page 16)

Having a clear filter also gives your business an identity and this is helpful when creating more systems for your business which lead to business growth. For more in depth information on the marketing filter I would recommend you get registered for the next Marketing Funnel class through www.handymanjourney.com

Marketing Filter Diagram
Figure 1

Your Marketing Message

Your Marketing Filter

Your Audience

Your
Marketing
Funnel

Marketing Funnel - Base Platform

There are many layers to marketing your business and the crazy part is that those layers are always changing with the seasons. The first step in creating a successful marketing strategy is having a base platform for your Marketing Funnel. The base platform of this Marketing Funnel is your professional website. You will note that I didn't just say "any normal website." You need a professional website that attracts the clients you are looking for.

Let's talk about Ideal Clients for a second, because the concept is critical when creating a website that attracts them. In a perfect world, the Ideal Client would be someone who is willing to pay what we are worth, is not in a hurry, is very loyal, and is willing to recommend our companies to family and friends. Truth is this client is very hard to find, but it is possible. You want your website, the base platform for your Marketing Funnel, to reflect that you are looking for that Ideal Client. Psychologically speaking, there is a lot that goes through someone's mind when they see a well put together, professional website rather than a website that was just thrown together. When you have a crisp and clean website that is designed with purpose, it attracts that Ideal Client and the not-ideal clients can tell that you might be of a higher standard than they are looking for. At the end of the day, this is business, not personal. Sometimes when people need a quick slap together fix and aren't willing to pay a proper dollar for it, there is no harm in recognizing the fact that you may not be able to help them with the work they need done because their budget does not match your work.

Another key thing about having a professional website is that the website has a clean and easy work request capturing platform. This allows the client to reach out to you via email and tell you exactly what they need done and even leave pictures at any time of the day or night. This also allows you to do the work you need to do throughout the day and not have to rely on answering your phone as it rings off the hook. The email capture allows you to get back to clients whenever it is convenient for you.

Another amazing use of the email capture on a website is that it allows you to regain leads that have fallen out of your Marketing Funnel through email blast marketing or even targeted marketing on Facebook or other forms of social media. All around, the base platform is a must, as it is the hinge that everything else in a marketing platform rides on!

Marketing Funnel - Outer Platforms

The outer platforms of the Marketing Funnel are just as important as the base platform, but they add more chaos in connecting to leads if the outer platforms are done without the base platform. For visual learners, I've included the diagram below on page 13 to further explain (Fig. 2 pg. 24). The outer platforms in the funnel are created by marketing platforms, such as Yelp, Google, Facebook, Home Advisor, etc. Later in this book, we will go further in depth on which one of these marketing platforms work best for your particular area, but for right now let's keep talking about the outer platforms and how they correlate with the base platform of the funnel.

Whenever you advertise on one of these platforms, it is essential to have your Ideal Client in mind when creating your advertisement. It is also important to make sure that when those Ideal Clients find you through that advertisement they can easily be directed to your base platform of your funnel (your website).

For instance, when creating your advertisement you will be asked what type of engagement you are looking for. For this to work correctly you will want to select "engagement on your website". This will set the ad to direct people to your base platform of your funnel so that the funnel can work correctly. When people find you on the outer platforms of the marketing funnel and are directed to your base platform (website), and fill out a work request form that is then sent to your email. You have successfully mitigated that client from calling you and taking you away from the work at hand.

However, you have still made it so that the client has reached out to you and you have secured that cold lead without you having to do any work.

That is really what this is all about: setting up systems in your business that will run without you, so that you can focus on the things that actually bring you more money. Imagine being able to focus on the job that you need to do and then opening up your email at lunch or once you finish up your job, and it is full of qualified leads just waiting for you to set up appointments. We all know what it is like to do the opposite: when you are trying to get work done and every 30 minutes to an hour the phone rings and you have to stop what you are doing to secure that lead, and you have no clue that that lead is a good lead or not until you talk with them. This is the reason why every handyman needs a Marketing Funnel.

Base Marketing Funnel Diagram
Figure 2

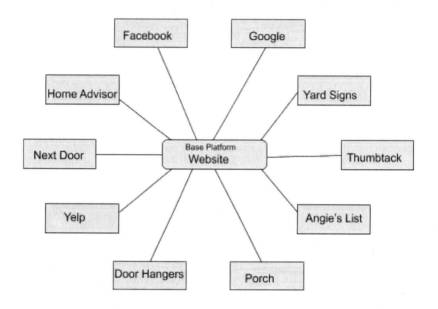

Marketing Funnel - Advanced Version

Once your handyman business grows a bit you have options. One thing that handymen don't have much of is time, so what I opted to do after about 2 years in business was to hire a part-time customer relations personnel. Creating this position really changed the whole face of my business and launched a whole new chapter of the handyman industry for me. The roles of the customer relations personnel are to answer phone calls, respond to email work requests that came from my website, follow up with past clients and send thank you / birthday cards out to clients. Having this CR personnel really changed the way I could look at my Marketing Funnel. I am no longer bound to sending potential clients to my website. I can now send them to our business phone number since the CR personnel would be there to answer the phone and set up appointments. This changed the funnel a bit. Now our base platform is our CR personnel and the two platforms beyond that are our phone and website, and then further, we have the traditional outer platforms (see Fig. 3 on pg. 29).

This restructure of the Marketing Funnel not only made our business more efficient, but it made us more professional and ultimately more profitable. When I am not glued to the phone all day, I can complete the repairs quicker and have time to focus on growing the business. This has led to improved systems I have created in our business to help it be more efficient yet. This also led to hiring additional handyman employees.

There is great power in structuring your business marketing with the Marketing Funnel by ultimately helping you to become a more efficient business. This leads to more profits, which leads to more investment into those things that grow the business, which leads to business growth and more profits yet.

This restructuring of the funnel has currently made it where I have now moved to another position in my company. I am currently the estimator. The CR personnel receives all the calls and emails and then sets appointments for me to come out and inspect the property and write them an estimate. Then, once the estimate is accepted, that gets sent over to our technician who then calls the client and sets an appointment for work. Once work is completed, the CR personnel follows up with the client, usually 2-3 weeks after the job, sends a thank you card, and the whole system starts over again.

As you can see, you have the resources to make your business work hard without having to rip your hair out. It's all in the funnel and the systems that you create in your business! One book that I would highly recommend you read regarding structuring your business for growth and creating systems in your business so that it runs smoothly with minimal work is The E-Myth Revisited by Michael Gerber. This book has changed my business outlook forever, and I am sure it will do the same for you.

Advanced Marketing Funnel Diagram
Figure 3

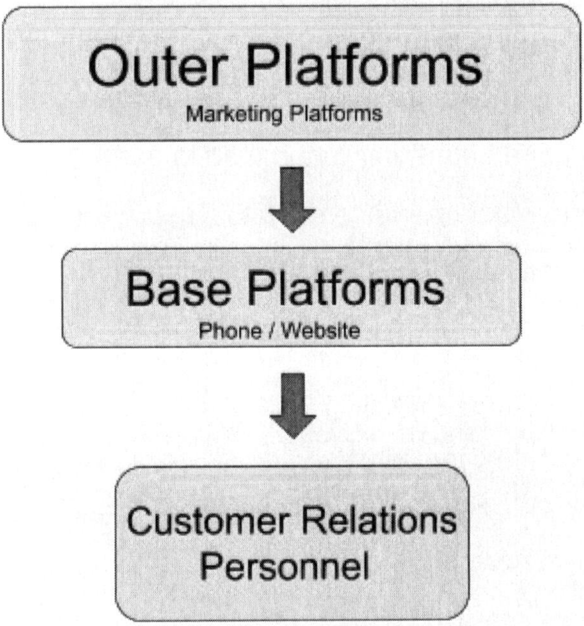

Outer Platforms
Marketing Platforms

Base Platforms
Phone / Website

Customer Relations Personnel

Which marketing Platforms work best in your area

"Which marketing platform works best in my area?" or "How should I advertise?" are two of the most common questions I have received in my years of handyman business consulting. The answer is fairly complicated because there is no one marketing platform that works for everyone everywhere all the time. It's quite entertaining because in our Handyman Mastermind group on Facebook, someone will post that they have had great success with Yelp and at least a dozen other people will chime in and say that Yelp is a rip off. So is Yelp a rip off or the best thing since the claw hammer? Well, it's both, depending on where you are located and who you are advertising to.

More often than not most handymen that are struggling to find work are simply advertising in the wrong way and possibly to the wrong demographic. There are many different ways to find what advertising platform works best in your area, but in this book I am going to share with you personal experience and ways that I have found worked for me to find out what works best in your area. These tips have helped many people all around the world find out how to engage with their Ideal Clients and start making more money!

There are multiple layers of finding out which platform works best for you, so it takes time. This is not a get rich quick scheme (those don't exist), so if you are ready for some trial and error work then follow these steps to find out which marketing platform works best in your area.

Start by typing in "handyman near (your town)" into Google or whatever search engine you use. This will bring up many results, and what we are currently interested in is the first result that comes up after all the ads. So for instance, if I type in "Handyman near Sacramento", the first website that gets displayed after all the ads is Yelp. This gives me a great indication that Yelp is used quite often in Sacramento and that it might be a great place to advertise. Now you have to think about all the Ads you saw when you searched for this. Google is currently the #1 most searched site on the internet so even before Yelp, Google is a better place to advertise. It all depends on how the majority of people in your area view ads.

I have a friend that whenever he searches for something he skips all the "ads" and goes to the first organic site that comes up. In his mind he wants an organic search that people are at the top due to ratings not because they bought that slot. So you have to know your clientele: are they the type of people who skip the "ads" or do they just go for the first one they see? A lot of this only comes through trial and error.

Some great words of wisdom in this is "it takes money to make money". You need to experiment a little and find out what works best for you, but this searching tip gives you a great idea of where to start. Using the search engine approach is exactly how I did things when I was looking to create the outer platforms of my marketing platform.

The next thing you will look into is if people around your area frequently use Facebook or other social media platforms like Nextdoor. If so, then you need to advertise there. Some more high end areas prefer to use word of mouth or local businesses.

For these areas, I have found door to door flyers or yard signs very effective.

I always recommend at least starting out with a base platform (website) and at least one outer platform (see Fig. 1). My first was Yelp, in which you are advertising on a monthly basis. Once your business begins to grow, the common natural reaction would be to decrease your advertising since you feel like you have plenty of work and are steadily busy. In the world of business completely cutting off your advertising can be a killer.

As your business grows, I recommend that you up your marketing outer platforms to at least one additional platform. I currently have 4 outer platforms and these include Yelp, Facebook, Google, and yard signs. I have found that Facebook works really well at capturing people that didn't even know they needed handyman work. I have had many people tell me that they were just scrolling through Facebook, saw my ad, got to thinking if they needed any work. They magically came up with stuff, and the more they thought about it, the more they wanted that work done. This is the whole goal of marketing just like we mentioned earlier. The goal of marketing is to capture and mold the prospect's mind. The more platforms that you can do this on, the better. It's the same in political campaigns. When most people go to the polls, they look through the names of the candidates and the name that seems the most familiar is the one they tend to vote for; this is called name recognition. More often than not those candidates had more advertisements than the others that were seen by the voter. This is the goal of marketing.

Yelp

When I first started my handyman business years ago, Yelp was my first addition to my outer platform of my Marketing Funnel. I advertised on Yelp for 4 months for $300 per month. They had a free $300 coupon, so that is originally why I went with them. Through the years, I have advertised on and off with Yelp but now I have a running ad on Yelp for $250 per month and keep that going all the time. I started paying Yelp every month because it works, and it turns out that it is the best way to advertise in my area. It is a very cost effective form of advertising if it works for you.

The best way to get started with Yelp ads is to give Yelp a call. Thatis, if they haven't called you already! On the Yelp website you can submit an ad request and they will have someone reach out to you soon to set something up. For starters, I would recommend getting ads for as much as you can afford, even if that is only $50, I would start there. Make sure you ask them if they are running any ad promotionals at the moment. They will usually be happy to give you a discount to get a new customer. When I started I received a $300 in free ads coupon. Remember, marketing is one of the best investments for your business, so don't be afraid to spend money in this area.

Google

Advertising with Google is fairly new to me. Honestly, I don't know why I didn't start it earlier. I like the breakdown of impressions and clicks per dollar spent, and it is proving to be a great form of advertising in my area. The ad I pay for on Google is $350 per month in my area, and it shows an ad to people that I designate. Currently, I have it set for a certain age group of people that live in the 3 surrounding cities of me.

One thing about Google, Like many other platforms, is that people can send you an estimate request through your Google business page or better yet you can direct them to submit a work request through your website and thus stick to the Marketing Funnel!

To get ads started on Google you will need to go to ads.google.com and follow their prompts on getting started. They also have people that you can call that will help you through the process if needed.

Facebook

I have tinkered around with Facebook advertising from time to time throughout the years, but just recently ramped it up to every month. I currently pay $350 per month for Facebook ads. Like Google, Facebook has a tool where you can direct the ads to people in a certain age group and demographics. I hear from clients frequently that they saw an ad on Facebook and it got them thinking about what they needed done around their home! This is the goal!

Facebook is a fun ad to start, in my mind at least, because you get to see how your audience reacts to it. At the end of the day it's not super hard to start a Facebook ad but the trick is to do it so it is engaging and geared towards the right people. I would recommend you reach out to my marketing professional, Jason Call, at

www.handymanwebdesign.com. He is a master at SEO optimizing ads and can get you started on the right track with this. Remember what I said, sometimes it is best to hire someone to do the things that you don't understand. This is one of those times!

Some free ways to "market" yourself on Facebook is to create a free Facebook page for your business and post daily! This is important because it builds consistency. Another great way is to join local Facebook groups and be a helpful person and recommend your services in a professional manner whenever someone is in need. If you create a good reputation for yourself others will share your name on these groups without you even asking!

Yard Signs / Door Hangers

Yard signs for me are also a fairly new addition to my outer platforms. I created a design that I liked, shared it in The Handyman Journey mastermind group on Facebook, and got some great feedback on the design and layout of it. I finalized a design and had them ordered from VistaPrint. It cost me $14.25 per sign and the stakes for the sign were $.83 a piece on Amazon. The signs have been a fantastic addition to our marketing platform because when they are placed in clients yards, they are essentially a personal referral that their neighbors see every day on their way home from work! We typically put up yard signs at homes when we finish the work and ask if they can be left up for about 3 - 4 weeks and typically the clients are more than happy to help us that way. When creating your yard signs or door hangers, you want to figure out whether you want to put your website on there or your phone number. Ultimately, I think this comes down to if you are taking all the calls personally or if you have a CR personnel. If you have someone at the office to take calls then I would put your phone number on the signs. If you do not have someone in the office, then I would recommend you putting your website on the signs. Placing yard signs throughout town has kept our business busier than ever.

The key to yard signs is the graphics. You don't want too much on your sign so it looks crowded but you want enough on there that people get the point of what you do and how to contact you. In my mind, all you need on a yard sign is "Home Repairs By: and then your logo and then your number or website". Remember to check local laws for advertising as a handyman. For instance, my signs say "not a licensed contractor" per the California

Contractor Board. I would recommend reaching out to people you know and see if anyone has a background in graphics that might be able to help. A graphic designer is another valuable investment in this business as your logo is the first thing customers see and can make a good or bad impression on your business. If you are struggling to find someone who can help, check out 'The Handyman Journey Mastermind' group on Facebook! There are a lot of great guys on there that specialize in all kinds of things besides home repairs and can give you some great advice!

NextDoor

Nextdoor is an online social media platform that is a great resource for advertising your business. Nextdoor does not currently have any paid advertisement function, but since it is a neighborhood based site, it is a great space for personal referrals. Nextdoor is a great referral system used by the elderly population who may not be on Facebook. Here they can ask their neighbors who they have trusted to come into their home and give them superior service.

Nextdoor is an easy website to join, simply go to www.nextdoor.com and create an account and start sharing what you do when people are in need of home repairs!

Conclusion

The marketing platforms that I have talked about here are ones that I have particularly had experience with and have experienced positive results. There are many platforms that I did not talk about because I do not have personal experience with them. I know people who have had great results with the other platforms, but I also know many who have had poor results. Again these platforms vary from place to place. Also keep in mind that even the different towns around you may have different marketing platforms that work better than others.

In conclusion, this book is composed of tips that have helped people make millions of dollars in their handyman business all around the world and my hope would be that it does the same for you. It is my honor to get to share this information with you and I am really excited to hear how you put this into practice. Leave us a message to let us know how this book has influenced your business at www.handymanjourney.com.

Your next step Resources:

-   If you are looking for more in depth applied information on these Marketing Funnels I would recommend you sign up for the Marketing Funnel class through www.HandymanJourney.com We have had dozens of handymen go through this class and their business have absolutely exploded due to applying this content! You can also see some testimonials at www.handymanjourney.com

- Visit www.handymanjourney.com
  where there are countless resources
  from e-books to full blown courses on
  many topics that you can take to take
  your handyman business to the next
  level!

- Visit www.handymanwebdesign.com
  and see how Jason Call can help you
  out. Mention that Allen Lee sent you!

- Follow The Handyman Journey on
  Youtube, Instagram, and Facebook to
  follow along on our Handyman
  Journey.

Youtube:

https://www.youtube.com/channel/UCHO4P
h5ithDRTski0RA0wlw

Facebook:

https://www.facebook.com/HandymanJourn
ey/

Instagram:

https://www.instagram.com/the_handyman_
journey/

- Join the conversation about others
  handyman journey on The Handyman
  Journey mastermind group on
  facebook at
  https://www.facebook.com/groups/955
  093931316242/

Made in United States
Cleveland, OH
30 December 2024

12846522R00030